"I wish I had a brother like Jake!"

Steven Holmes…..UVA, NCAA, Defensive MVP and currently playing for both the Denver Outlaws of MLL and the Philadelphia Wings of NLL.

JAKE JENNINGS:
LACROSSE GOALIE

Jake Jennings: Lacrosse Goalie

By: Lisa Butler

Illustrated By: J.D. Whitman

To Isabel, Aidan and Lily.
Have fun with your own game!
Lisa Butler

**The
Payne Press**

Copyright © 2012 by Lisa Butler.

For information about special discounts for
bulk purchases please contact The Payne Press,
670 Penllyn Blue Bell Pike, Blue Bell, PA 19422

Composed by M&K Publishing, Hobe Sound, FL

Manufactured by Color House Graphics, Inc.,

Grand Rapids, MI, USA

October 2012

Job #38445

Printed in the United States of America.

Library of Congress Control Number 2012913812

ISBN 97080985825031

Note: This book is printed on 30% postconsumer
recycled paper and is SFI (Sustainable Forestry
Initiative) certified. The ink is vegetable based, not
petroleum based.

This book is dedicated to my three awesome boys and their amazing friends.

Jake Jennings: Lacrosse Goalie

ONE

Team Jennings

Finally here. My first season. I'm so stoked. At last something to make fourth grade mildly bearable: Seven weeks, seven games and one tournament make the wait worth it. Thank you for the best thing since June, July and August.

I am no lacrosse newbie. Charlie and Henry (my two older brothers) play, and man, can they kick your you know what! And luckily for me, they've been using me as a human backstop ever since I was shorter than most lacrosse sticks and wouldn't cry if I got hurt. Actually, my first stick and I may have been holding each other up.

Anyways, like everything else important in life, my brothers clued me in about lacrosse, but even they don't know the answers to my super secret questions: Will I have to play goalie like Charlie and face the firing squad of machine gun shots to my head? And, do I have the nerve to tell Charlie that I'm not sure I have the nerve to play goalie?

Playing goalie is totally not cool. Sure Charlie plays that position, so naturally he really wants me to play too, but to play goalie would be like the worst nightmare ever. Make that playing goalie is already my worst nightmare. That rubber ball is hard; it could really mess someone's face up. Like mine. Guys park five feet from the crease and fire the ball at the goalie's head at over fifty miles per hour. Yikes. And, goalies have to pay attention. Something I haven't exactly starred in so far. Even worse, people notice if you mess up. Besides, I really want to score goals, and I'd prefer, thank you very much, to just skip the part about getting blamed for the team losing.

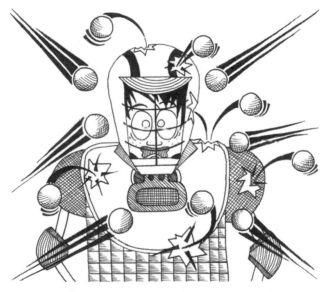

That rots big time—just way too much heat in the goalie kitchen. No thanks.

But don't even start with calling me a wimp about this goalie thing because I'm not. There is no nightlight in my room, I can squish a live spider between two fingers and I can catch frogs and lizards with my bare hands! My friends call me J.J., and I really don't care which of the J's from Jake Jasper Jennings the J.J. comes from. My two brothers are Henry who is 15 and Charlie who is 13. My dog, Yamaha is six, but actually, that's like 42. You figure it out. My friends get on my case for talking a lot, but I could care less because I have a lot to say. My older brothers are actually pretty cool sometimes. Ok, we fight a lot, but we're just brothers, that's just the way it is, and it's kind of fun. We laugh a lot too. Yeah, we're a team. Don't mess with the Jennings three!

TWO

Knight Time

I keep my lax stick under the bed with my light saber. Just hearing the names of the sticks will hook you because what the companies call them is mean sounding names like "Maverick" or "Warrior." You get to pick a head and a shaft to make your own wicked weapon. Charlie plays with the Proton Power head and Wonder Boy shaft. Henry plays with the Clutch head and Kryptolight shaft. Their sticks are seriously bad. Oh yeah, no more pirate swords for me.

My hand-me-down stick is so old the names have worn off, but I'm pretty sure it could have been a Revolver/Gnarr or Blade/ Swizzbeat. The old stick is pretty much a joke but still it's a real stick and it's in my hands. It's my new wand, and I'm going to make some lax magic!

So, I'm off to the garage in search of this season's old cleats from the huge bin, that's the dump for all of my brothers' old sports junk. I find some smelly pads there too. I've also got to dig for shoulder pads, elbow pads, helmet, mouth guard, and gloves. No, forget the mouth guard; there's a limit to the whole hand-me-down tradition. Like a knight preparing for battle, I pull the tag, snap, and then buckle until the armor feels fit for battle. My reflection stares back at me from the window of Mom's mini-van. Sigh. Unlike a knight, there's no shine on my armor. It's mud-crusted and smells like my brothers' dirty clothes basket. So why does it feel so right?

Here comes Henry to inspect me. He looks at me like I'm a plate full of broccoli. Then, like a worm after a rain storm, a grin crawls across his face. "Look at you, Jake. You newb. Think you're

ready for the first practice? Let me give you a hint."

I hate the know-it-all Henry hints, but I hate even more how they're almost always right.

"Okay squirt. First off, you put your equipment on at the field, not at home," he says like he's Joe-Varsity star. "Take it all off and stack it on your stick like this. Like a game of ring toss, Henry drops my equipment onto my stick: helmet first, then shoulder pads, gloves and elbow pads. Order obviously matters. The gear slides down and then stops at the head of the stick—all squished together. Then swinging the stick up over his shoulder he says; "Now that's the way to do it."

"Got it," I respond.

And I did have it. I hate to do what he says, but now I do feel cool.

"Yeah and don't forget that coaches really love it when…," but he doesn't finish because he gets a text. Henry's all about his phone and girls. The two are definitely related. Henry's girl thing bothered me at first, but now I have to admit it's getting kind of interesting.

"Hey, and don't forget your cup," Henry laughs as he walks away. Another place I'm drawing the line on hand-me-downs.

Dad says the most important piece of equipment is the cup. Mom says it's the helmet. I usually agree with Mom, but in this case, probably not. My mom actually giggles when she gives me my cup. Oh brother. But there it is, and it's blue! Mom marks mine with a Sharpie and writes a J for me, Jake Jasper Jennings. It makes me wonder why. Is cup theft really an actual problem? Cup is a dumb name for the things. Talk about something you'll never drink out of! Tomorrow is our first practice.

THREE

Goalie and the Mikey Blues

At the field for our first practice I see my best friends; Troy and Ricky are already catching and throwing. Ricky is going to be a total lax stud. He is already famous because his dad played for our school and people call him "The Legend." He is in the Athletic Hall of Fame for both lacrosse and soccer. He has a ton of trophies!

Troy is tall, and skinny, and don't ask me why, but he's always hungry. He sniffs around for food more than a bear at a picnic! Troy and I were actually born on the same day. No question we had to be best friends from day one. I think that's some kind of birthday rule or something? The rule after the one where you get to choose your cake. You gotta have the right cake.

Feeling pretty impressive, I'm carrying my equipment over my shoulder just like Henry showed me. I look up and there is a crowd of kids around Mikey. That kid always gets everything he wants. I mean it's like it's his birthday every week. He's always got something new to show off. And, boy does he show it off. One week, it's that slick new backpack on wheels, then it's that new Mario game for the computer, then it's his brand new Gecko named Vandal (yup named after his stick). The thing is, it's not dumb stuff, it's all really cool, and unfortunately he knows it. And, he has to tell you about all the latest loot which just makes you mad even before he opens his mouth. Now that he is on our team, guess I'll have to hear constantly about all of his stuff.

"Looks like another fun season with Mikey," I say to Ricky and Troy sarcastically. "What's the latest?"

"Some jersey that's signed by some star lacrosse player," Troy says.

"I hate his spoiled guts," Ricky adds.

I'm trying so hard not to look at the

signed jersey that I don't even realize that I've stuck my fingers through a hole in my faded, ripped, worn-by-Henry-or-Charlie, very old jersey. To take our minds off the Mikey factor, we gear up, and then Ricky, Troy and I all start hitting each other. "Checking" it's called in lacrosse. Bumping into each other with all of this padding on is fun and made sweeter without Mikey in our circle.

The Coach blows his whistle. "Okay guys, line up over here," he calls. Mom told me his name, but I already forget. It doesn't matter anyway. Coaches like to be called "Coach", especially if they're the kind who has to wear a suit and tie all day.

"Welcome to your first practice of your first season of lacrosse. I'm Coach Morgan and the name of our team is the Chiefs. Today, we'll start by taping

your names on the front of your helmets. That way I'll know who you are and so will your teammates. We'll also run a safety check to see that all of your equipment is on the right way. And then we'll do some stick handling, passing and catching, begin the basics of dodging, talk about field positions and finish the practice off by running a few sprints."

Ok, I think, so far, so good. The guy seems to have a clue.

"After we're labeled with tape, we all stand in a circle for the safety check. Then, MORE cup stuff! He makes us show our mouth guards, no big deal, but then we have to tap on our cups with our sticks. Before you know it, every kid is banging on their cups. It's like a little drum band on the lacrosse field. I like to think of myself as hard to embarrass, but team cup tapping is a bit much.

After the safety check is finally over we do a bunch of passes. I think it's harder to catch than throw, but I'm solid with both. Good thing all that backyard lax pays off. I'm feeling pretty good, and cup tapping is off the screen completely.

Next we work on field positions. As if we didn't already know, Coach explains there are nine players plus the goalie in three lines of players; three attack, three middies and three defenders. Only six guys can play on one side of the field at one time or they're "off-sides." I'm thinking I'm pretty cool just to be out there on the field until Coach barks in his tough-guy voice that it's time for sprints. No! Of course, Ricky, "Boy Wonder," beats us all. He's ultra fast. Troy and I race, but he beats me too. But wait, I look behind me. There's Mikey. Yes, I beat him, but inside I know that beating Mikey isn't much better than beating the girls who put mirrors in their lockers. My dreams of playing attack may become just that, pure dream.

"Okay guys, great first practice,"
Coach says. "Next week, we'll talk more
about positions; you'll each have a chance to
experiment with all of them. Before you leave, I
have your Chiefs jerseys."

Did he really say ALL positions; does
that include goalie? Just the way he said
"experiment" makes me think that being in
goal is like a freaky science thing—like let's
just throw them in there and watch to see what
happens! Like when you put a piranha in a
goldfish tank. You know, that doesn't end up so
well for the goldfish.

We all couldn't wait to see our new jerseys. They are blue with a gold Chief.

"Coach," Mikey shouts with his hand up before any of us even thought we had a choice. "Can I have number 1? It's my lucky number."

"Okay, Mikey," Coach says in kind of a tired sounding voice that shows he's already on to Mikey. Then every hand is up.

"Coach, can I have number three, Coach can I have number 20?" It keeps going. That Mikey is always stirring up something.

Then Coach showed us the special stick and extra pads we would use when (not if) we played goalie. Okay, so I'm getting more and more worried about how serious Coach is about this goalie thing!

Anyway, I just take what's left, number 33. Still, I'm pretty pumped that we ALL, not just Mikey, have new jerseys. Mine feels totally sharp. Can you say, "Lax Dude"?

FOUR

Sticks and Strings

"Hey, was that your buddy Ben using a girl's stick at practice?" my brother Charlie asks through a stream of snickering. He's totally cracking himself up. It's like he thinks he's making fun of me when it really was poor Ben who showed up at practice with a girls' stick. Admittedly, Ben is on the clueless side, but hey, the guy has three sisters. His mother didn't know better. She just gave him one of their sticks. At least the strings weren't pink. I just feel so sorry for the guy, with three sisters, what does he do for fun?

"So," I glare at Charlie with my hate-you stare.

"You're so lame," he says. "You really don't know anything about lacrosse. And, you really won't until you start playing goalie. Then you'll feel the rush."

"I do too," I say. "And, you are so not the boss of me!"

"Yes, I am. And you know it little guy."

He is so mean.

Boys' lacrosse sticks have strings in them, like a net, which form a pocket. Special strings weave through the pocket called shooting strings, which I am about to learn more about. Apparently these special strings improve your shooting.

"You know you need new shooting strings on that head of yours," Charlie informs me.

How would I know that? My stick is actually Charlie's old one from before Charlie started playing goalie. He keeps telling me what an honor it is to get to use his old stuff. What a load of you-know-what. I'd like to see him using hand-me-downs!

"What's wrong with it?" The words sneak out of my mouth without permission. I'm actually afraid to ask.

"You're such a newb, Jake," Charlie says laughing at me. Newb is his favorite word. I hate how much he loves it.

"You know you're throwing the ball down because of your little string problem," Charlie instructs me. In fact I didn't even know that I was throwing the ball down, but I was not going to let on. Question to self: Couldn't someone have told me this before now?

"How would I know? You guys never let me touch your sticks," I say.

"Why would we," Charlie says as he grabs my stick from me.

"Dude, what the heck?"

"Just let me see it," Charlie insists. He barely looks at it and says, "This thing is all wrong." Then he starts pulling at the strings like it's his stick again.

"Yo J.J., I think your pocket is illegal, too. The ball can't sit that low in your stick."

Pocket, illegal? Another thing about the stick I didn't know. I'm feeling stupider by the minute.

"Hey, stop, what are you doing, it's mine."

"Nah, it's still mine, so just cool your jets Junior. I'm just gonna string it right," he informs me as he begins twisting, pulling and poking the strings.

I watch him and wonder. Even though I'm furious, I wonder why he is being nice to me. Something to consider. He never helps me with anything, so there must be something in it for him. Uh oh, what does he want? Once before he made me be his personal butler, and I had to get him whatever he asked for. Never again. But I'm wrong. Turns out he's just psyched to try something new with the strings, but, of course, he wouldn't experiment on his own stick! The next thing I know, he's got all the strings out of the head of my stick.

"I don't know how you can play with this piece of junk anyway," he says.

"Yeah, well guess what? You made it a piece of junk." One of my best ever comebacks. I'm feeling smarter, but he doesn't care.

"You're so clueless," Charlie says.

Charlie restrings the whole thing, but says again that I need new shooting strings. My mom says that I have to use my allowance money to buy them. This seems crazy since an hour ago I had a stick that seemed to work fine to me. So off we go to the lacrosse store where at least I can pick a new color for the strings. I go with yellow, because it's the closest color to the Chief on our jerseys.

Mr. Ferris, the store owner, looks over my stick, turning it over and over in his hands, eyeing it like it's some alien death sword from outer space. He chuckles, "this stick has been around a while. I think it's an old Proton with a Krypto shaft, hard to tell. But it's a classic for sure. Son, this is really a mess. These strings are all twisted up like a bird's nest. I'm thinking I need to start from the beginning and restring the whole thing."

Now I'm really steaming mad at Charlie. He took apart a perfectly good stick, made me spend five bucks on new strings, and now it's not a lacrosse head; it's a bird's nest! There is good news though. Mr. Ferris says that if I buy the strings from him, he'll restring it for free. An hour later, I'm flat broke, but boy does he ever fix it. Wow, it looks fierce! Plus, it's a classic, which sounds impressive.

"Bummer for you, Jake. At least you got a half decent stick out of it," Charlie says. In the car it hits me that my older brother actually almost tried to apologize to me. And meant it too. He might even have tried to help me. Weird, but true.

At dinner, we tell Dad the whole story. My Dad is really smart. He always thinks about things before he talks, but we don't usually listen. I know we should. He thinks. We're silent, waiting.

"You know guys, it's not about the equipment, it's really about the player," he says.

"Makes sense to me," I say, as I am wondering if Mikey's Dad ever says the same thing.

Henry and Charlie just give me the "you're too unimportant to care about" stare.

"How was your first practice?" Dad asks.

"Minus the Mikey factor, awesome. Troy and Ricky are playing too! I got number thirty-three," I respond.

"So Jake, when do you start goalie training," Charlie asks?

Here it comes, the big sales job from Charlie. He thinks goalie is the toughest position on the field, but NO WAY. I mean it's just a death wish to want to stand in the path of rubber rocks shot from sticks with intent to maim, or at least, score a goal.

"Give him time," my Dad answers for me, but what's he mean? That after a while I'll come around to seeing the point of being a human target?

As pathetic and scary as Charlie's goal-centered world seems, I still don't want to tell him playing goal is almost last on my list, just before riding the bench and just after playing the pixie harp. Just because it's a brother's job to be a jerk doesn't mean the brotherhood doesn't matter, and pathetically, I don't want to let him down.

FIVE

Game #1 - Refs, Lectures, and Goals

I wake up, it's Saturday. Our first lacrosse game. I'm so pumped! I feel like the blood's going to burst from my veins. Heaven help the poor guy in the net. I'm actually hoping to SCORE some goals, not BLOCK goals!

"Hey J.J., big deal, huh—first game and all," Henry says running by me in the hall and whacking me on the back just hard enough that it really hurts, but not hard enough that I can complain. Brotherly love? Nope. It's just random pain courtesy of Henry because he's older, because he's bigger, because he can. At least the game day buzz kills the sting.

"Yo, bobble head, gonna win today or what?" he asks. He's the one that actually looks like a bobble head (probably got the insult from looking in the mirror), but could I ever say that? No way! Well maybe, and then die young. Choosing life, I keep a civil tongue in my head, but that head is also spinning mad.

"Stop it, stop it, and STOP IT." But I know from how pathetically weak the words sound that I've surrendered again.

"Ladies, ladies, save your arguments for the Hello Kitty party," my father says. He can't stand it when we bicker with each other like that. He says we're acting like a bunch of little girls so he calls us ladies. I don't care, but it really gets to my brothers which actually make it very funny for me.

"DAAAAD!" my brothers yell at him.

Then Mom swoops in at super sonic speed, "Let's go, let's go. Jake, do you have your water bottle? Everyone in the car, now at the latest!"

"Mom do we really HAVE to go to his game?" Henry whines. "These kid games are as boring as watching grass grow. They can't even catch, much less shoot. How is the little thinks-he's-a-hot-shot going to play the field when his only experience is blocking our shots- ha, or should I say, not blocking them?"

"Yeah, like how much does it matter if he's not in goal?" Charlie grumbles.

"Get in the car," Mom says. Whew, another goalie conversation avoided!

"Mom, come on. This is pathetic. We're just staying home. I'm supposed to meet Josh on an X-Box Live game right now."

Mom wants them to come. They'd rather shove toothpicks under their nails. I'm happy thinking of them ripping each other to shreds instead of me.

"Yes, you do have to go to his game. Your brother has been at your games since the day he came home from the hospital. You are going, so get in the car."

Yeah, they know Mom is totally right, so I don't say anything. No need to.

Henry comes right up to me and says, "Don't let your head get any bigger because this is the last game I'm ever coming to." Luckily he's so tall that if I don't look up, he's just talking to the top of my head. I can ignore him if he can't see my eyes. Great trick.

We get to the field and Coach brings us all in for a huddle. Our game today is against the Sharks. Even though it's a fourth and fifth grade league, rumor has it that some Sharks are killers, plus gi-normous.

"Okay guys, I'll need someone to volunteer to play goalie. Who's ready today?" he asks.

I look around; it is so silent you can hear the tension. I'm looking at the ground. I lift my head just high enough to see everyone else is doing the same. No one wants to play goalie and we all know it, except Coach who now seems a little clueless.

"No one? Okay, no problem. I'll just pick," says Coach. "Remember, everyone will have a turn. AJ, you'll be up first. Gear up!" Bummer for him, but I'm feeling deep breathing relief at having dodged that bullet. Uh oh, it's not over.

"Jennings, didn't I hear that your brother plays goalie," Coach asks? I don't answer. I can't help it even though I picture steam coming out of Mom's ears. I can't even lift my head to look at Coach because that would suck me into a conversation about the goalie job. I just grab my stick and tear off as fast as I can to find Ricky or Troy.

We're passing and shooting to warm up, but still I can't focus. At the other end of the field, Coach is standing in front of A.J. who is in the goal. He is actually throwing the ball at A.J. We're mesmerized by the goalie training, and AJ seems downright frozen—he's playing slow-mo human target.

"Hey Coach, I'm not so sure about this!" A.J. screams. Thwack, another ball hits A.J.'s pads. "Ah Coach, I stink at this," he says.

"You're doing great A.J. Just watch the ball," Coach instructs. Thwack again, even louder.

It's horrible. A.J. is a regular piñata as ball after ball pounds his pads. I'd laugh but the whole scene is pretty pathetic. Maybe some candy will fall out of him. Then, Bam! This time the ball sounds real serious as it hits him right on his face mask.

"See, it doesn't hurt (which actually screams it really does hurt). Make sure you move your feet and get your body in front of it," Coach says. Great! Watch the ball, move your feet. With that advice at this speed AJ will be all set by, maybe Christmas.

Silently we all look at each other and slowly turn back to our warm up. AJ is making playing goalie look worse than I could have imagined it. I'm totally 100 percent fast-forwarding to the day when Coach picks me and starts rocketing balls at my head.

Time to line up. I'm starting on defense. Finally, the whistle blows and for a split second everything seems to stop. A Shark guy gets the ball first and he is coming right at me. Thanks to years of big brother boot camp drills, I know stopping a guy from getting a shot off is up to me. So, I charge right at him and dig my

shoulder right in his gut. Direct hit. He's down.
I'm down. Man I'm good. But the referee is
blowing his whistle like a wild man.

He points at me and says, "33, no body
checking in this league son. This is a warning.
Next time you'll have to serve a penalty. Take
it easy. And remember pal, three passes before
you shoot." Yeah, no more whistles for me, I
will remember.

So what's the point of all of this darn equipment if you can't body check? No time to answer, game on, the Sharks have the ball. Pass, pass again, and I'm on the guy like a bad haircut. I slap the ball to the ground. Six of us get on it at once, yelling at each other to get it! My dad claims the best way to get the ball out of a pack is to kick it, so I do and actually get the ball out. I pass it down to the offense. Now feeling smooth again!

By halftime the other team is winning 3-1. Back in the goal, poor A.J. looks like the principal just announced what a sweet boy he is at assembly. Now it's my turn on attack. Again we're swarming like bees out of a busted hive. The kick trick works again and I'm rewarded with the ball and run at the goal. I can feel the shot building up inside of me. For a few seconds it feels like I've got a fast-break. But the defender approaches. I respond with a quick pivot to my off-stick side, and bending low with my back to the guy, I swing around and accelerate. Roll dodge complete.

Then I hear Coach yelling, "Pass, J.J., pass the ball!"

I'd forgotten the darn three rule again. But before the defense can get me I pass off to Troy, who flips it to Jeff, who shovels it back to me and score. My first goal. Our chest bumps are downright explosive. Lacrosse rules and I LOVE IT!

We end up winning 5-3. Thanks to goals by Troy, Jeff, and me, and unfortunately two for Mikey. The Sharks weren't too big for us after all. Troy called them the Nurse Sharks! The season is off to a perfect start.

SIX

Dog Breath!

Tuesday, time for our second practice. I'm watching that so foul-it's-funny show on TV called *Dirty Jobs,* about totally gross stuff people do. You gotta love a program devoted to the disgusting side of life. Today there's a guy who's cleaning pig pens and he's just about to slip and wipe out right in all the pig poop. Right then, Henry blasts into the room, steals the clicker from me and starts his usual mindless channel clicking, which I refuse to call surfing, because no, he is no surfer. Even surfers are not that brain dead.

"Henry, what the bleep is your problem? I was totally watching that show," I say. Apparently clicker hogging is a right of the first born.

"Yeah, what are you going to do about it, go crying to your mommy? Oh look, I'm so scared. Just shaking like a leaf." He shakes his whole body like a spastic inchworm. Before I have to begin to fight back and lose, Mom mercifully calls. I manage to get off half a stare, but I can see from his "you're pathetic" stare that it's DOA.

"Let's go, Jake, turn off the TV and get your gear together. Time for practice," Mom yells from the kitchen.

I get up to leave, trying to seem like I'm sorry I have to go, but before I do, I fire a pillow like a Frisbee at Henry. A cheap shot, yes, but it's a direct hit. I can't resist whispering "jerk" under my breath, but I'm careful to be most of the way out of the door before I do.

I know where I have to go first—the laundry room for the cup. I paw through the basket; I can't believe it. No cup with a "J" on it. It can't be missing. I begin to wonder if

I'm headed down the same path as my brother who loses everything. No, I can't sink that low. I start my own search. As I'm getting more and more frantic, I look in the mud room, the basement, the family room, my room, the garage…no cup!

"Come on Jake, time to go. We're going to be late," Mom says. She's starting into that bad-cop tone she gets when it's time to go, really, finally. Mom's standard time is always really fast so I know I still have a little time.

Yamaha, our dog is following me everywhere on my search. Isn't that the coolest name? When we lived in Florida, we had a boat with a Yamaha outboard. Since when his tail starts wagging, it twirls around like the propeller on the engine, we named our dog after the engine. He follows us all of the time and I know he wants me to pet him, but I'm trying to ignore him. Still, he's hard to ignore and he knows it.

"Not now, buddy. I have to find my cup." Enter the cup-angel. A miracle occurs. I look down and what does Yamaha have in his mouth but my cup!

Yuck, that's so gross! Dog slobber on my cup is thoroughly gross, but what part of a cup's life isn't? I just grab it, not wanting to admit to

myself or anyone that my cup has been lost and then found in my dog's mouth.

I'm almost out the door when Charlie catches me.

"Jake, you gotta' be cool, man, be the goalie," Charlie's trying his hardest to make the word "goalie" sound as if it comes equipped with super powers.

"Aw Charlie, I don't know, it's my first season, I'm just thinking…..." that I really just don't know what to say.

"Come on J.J.– –Goalie is perfection. It's the real deal, because you're always plugged into the game," he says.

Oh great, I can just see myself plugged in so every time a ball gets fired at me, my hair would stand straight up, and my arms and legs would be vibrating like the cartoon of the dog with his paw in the socket! NO WAY!

"Jake, now," Mom calls. Her tone is bad-cop. Time has run out.

As I'm tossing my stuff in the car I've got that same sick feeling in my stomach that comes when Mom's trapping me in a lie. I guess that's because I am sort of lying to Charlie by not telling him straight up that I'd rather ride the bench than be standing in the goal.

We're at the park. I get out of the car just as Troy gets out, stuffing a granola bar in his mouth. Like a shark, he needs to constantly feed to stay in motion- he's always in motion.

SEVEN

Ground Ball Wars

Once again, kids crowd around Mikey. What now? I don't want to go, but I'm already on my way over to the crowd, sucked in just like the old saying about a moth to a flame. In this case, I wish Mikey was the flame and would just spontaneously combust. His latest jewelry is new cleats.

"Yeah, they're made just for lacrosse," he says. "My Dad ordered them online with our team colors. They're perfect for sharp cuts and fast breaks."

I turn to Troy and ask, "Are you kidding me? Special cleats?" I know I'm not sounding convincing to Troy because they actually look decidedly cool and scorching fast. I am so

wishing they were on my feet and not Mikey's, but I'll keep that jealousy to myself.

"That kid really needs to have the heck beaten out of him," Troy says. "But I don't want to chip a nail, so it'll have to wait. Let's go."

Coach runs out. I still can't remember his name, but calling him "Coach" is feeling more and more natural.

"Okay guys, bring it in," he says. "Today we're working on ground balls."

He shows us how not to rake the ball when it's on the ground, and shows us how to scoop it right into the stick by bending low with our knees, while keeping the stick low to the ground. He shows us how to cradle the ball by rolling the stick back and forth. We practice that for a while, and then he says it's time for a drill called "Ground Ball War." This sounds pretty intense.

Coach just smiles, like he knows that this is going to get good! Then he throws out fourteen balls, and there are fifteen of us. One of us isn't going to come up with a ball. Who is it going to be? He blows the whistle and we all dash out. We're all pushing to get a ball. I scoop one up. Phew, I'm safe for this round. I look up to see how Ricky and Troy did, they're good too. The next round he throws out thirteen balls for the fourteen of us who are left. This time I actually think about a strategy. Go to the outside, get the far ball! It works. I'm safe again.

Eventually, it's down to five kids and Coach now throws the four balls right to the center. So much for my outside strategy now! Ricky comes up empty. It's down to A.J.,

Mikey, Patel and me. All I think is I don't want
to get in Patel's path. The kid is huge, like he
should be in 7th grade. We call Patel "Tank".
He seems cool with it. He thinks it's funny.
We do too, but one shove from him and I'd be
flattened. Rushing in I kick a ball out. It works
like a charm, and I'm up with another ball
and still alive. It's down to the final three with
guess who? Tank, Mikey and me! No time
to think, I hear the whistle. Focus, Jake. But,
before I can even focus, whamo, I'm flat on my
back, looking up at the Tank's facemask. He's
crushed me. I'm out. Patel is in the finals with
Mikey. Dang, dang, dang! I'm more than a little
bummed.

Coach throws out the ball and Tank and
Mikey go for it. Patel may be bigger, but Mikey
is definitely faster. He dodges Tank and gets the
ball. Mikey wins. Those new cleats are looking
extra sharp, and I'm fighting off the thought that
they made the difference.

"Hey J.J., great job out there man, you almost had it," Ricky says as we're drinking some Gatorade. "Tough one against Tank. Ouch, pain central. Come on. Let's take some shots on goal."

I jam my bottle in my bag and run to catch up. It's great to have good buddies. I'm over my loss. As long as it's not goalie, it's all good for me! But just as I'm thinking that, a worry over what position I'll play in tomorrow's game pulls over my good mood like a big cloud that suddenly shuts off the sun at the beach. I'd be getting really depressed if an image of me rubbing Mikey's face in Troy's armpit didn't cheer me up.

EIGHT

Game #5–
Scoop the Poop!

We've played hard. We've tried hard. It's week five and I wish we could play forever. Game five is minutes away, and although I am already pumped, Coach's whistle bringing us in takes me up another notch. As my brothers would say, "The engine was redlining hot and I was about to drop the clutch."

"Today we are playing the Field Dogs," Coach says. "They started playing in 3rd grade, a year before us, so they are probably pretty good."

"Think you'll be captain today?" Ricky asks me as we're jogging in for the pre-game huddle.

"Probably not," I say, hoping that the dark magic of a bad prediction would work in my favor.

My hoping is cut short by Coach's pre-game strategy talk. These sessions remind me of my Dad who actually watches the pre-game shows for football. I'm like Dad; just call me in when they're ready for the kick off. Ditto here Coach; just call me in when we can start the game, right? But, here I can't escape the sermon—none of us can and here it comes!

"Okay guys, we're out here to play hard, but to have fun. So let's put our hearts and heads together and give it our all. Win those ground balls by getting low, especially with that back hand. You need short and quick passes and effective dodges. Cradle and set up good opportunities, no hot-dogging, and stay on your side of the field. Remember the off-sides rule: the defense doesn't cross the centerline to the attack side, and attack doesn't cross the centerline to the defense side. And remember too, boys, our experience playing the game is more important than whether we end up winning or losing the game. Jeff, you're up for goalie today, gear up! Ricky, you're captain. Go meet the ref."

Today, I've got some good news and some bad news: Good? I've made it another week without playing goalie. Whew. And Bad? I'm not captain, but Ricky is. And hey, that's as good as it gets if it can't be me!

Troy takes the face-off. In charge immediately, he gets the ball and we're off like firecrackers. I'm on "D" again. Troy goes down quickly and the Field Dogs collect the ball. The kid I'm guarding keeps trying to get around me and keeps stepping in the goal crease. Where is the referee? No attackers allowed in the crease! Field Dogs get two passes off, but drop the third. Ball down. My specialty! I charge into the pack. We're pushing and yelling to each other to get the ball, and that's when I hear it, or I should say, hear them. It's the parents.

The parents are all yelling like crazy, "Scoop, don't rake, go for the ball, let's go Chiefs, get tough!" Even normal parents, admittedly the exception, morph into yelling maniacs at a lacrosse game. They really do lose their grown-up calm and go wild.

Every time I hear them shout scoop, I think of scooping dog poop like we have to in the back yard. I just can't get that out of my head. Scoop – poop. Scoop-poop. Scoop-poop. The perfect rhyme.

The parents get so loud, that it's like they're inside our heads on the field instead of on the sidelines. It's all I hear, but then I remember to use my kick and scoop, and bingo, I'm up with the poop…uh, oh I mean ball. I manage to shoot a pass off to A.J. before being hacked by cheating-crease-guy. AJ catches and

throws to Mikey. It's one of the best feelings in the whole world to aim a pass, have it go where you want it to go, and have it caught. We're on it today! To Mikey, to Jeff. He shoots, he scores. We're up 1-0.

The flow continues; at the half, we're up 4-2. They shouldn't even have the two since that attacker keeps shooting from in the crease. Now I'm on attack, and we're all fired up! Of course, Mikey takes the face-off (put that on my wish list, too). He's got the ball. We're swarming, like bees, again, so I cut out to the left. Zing, it's fired to me, I'm running for the goal; it's in, score! But the referee is blowing his whistle like crazy, flapping his arms like a fat bird.

"No goal, no goal," he says.

What the heck? I'm getting the whistle again. Then, I remember; I did mess up, I forgot the three pass rule. All the glory wasted, major bummer. It's an epic failure. Maybe Henry and Charlie are right. Maybe I am pathetic. This game is hard: catching is hard, staying in position is hard, shooting is hard, and the three pass rule is really hard. Maybe I'm not actually a stud lax player in the making. But the play goes on.

The Field Dogs take the ball and whip it up the field. It crosses the midfield line, so I have to hang back; I'm not going to get called for off-sides. But thankfully the Field Dogs can't catch a thing, and we've got the ball again. It whizzes by me. I'm not paying attention again. I really blew it back there. Tank picks it up, gets it to Jimmy, to me, to Mikey. Mikey turns aggressively to the inside; he fakes left and goes right. He steps away hard exploding to the goal and he scores perfecting the inside-out dodge. The clock is ticking. I've got to concentrate now, just hoping that there is game time left for me to score. I really want to score! I really need to score.

Back to the face-off, and we've got it. I'm itching to get free, but the Field Dog covering me is too close. I do a quick V cut and get the pass. It's glory time. I shoot, but I miss. No goal, no glory. And, of course Mikey scores again. There is no justice. The kid never fails. I see my goal happening in my head, just not on the field. But hey, to shoot a little white ball past a goalie (who's double in size thanks to his gear) into a six foot net is tough. At least we won 6 – 2. But the Mikey factor being big in the win does bum me out me a little, even though I know it shouldn't.

Our record is now 4 and 1. And still, no goal duty for me! Thankfully, Charlie hasn't tortured me about it this week, but I know he won't let up for long. Nope, that train has left the station! He's relentless, but the real reason I hate his goalie push is that I'm scared—scared enough to not want the goalie subject even mentioned!

Scoop-poop. Scoop-poop. Scoop-poop.
It's like that great song on the radio that you just
can't stop singing! (And I'm still singing it.)

NINE

Goalie Practice

It has been raining so much this week that even our game was cancelled. I know for a fact that you can play lacrosse in the rain, but Coach said we'd trash the fields.

Oh well, Troy is coming over, that's a bonus. Charlie's friend Dan is already over and Henry's friend Josh is coming soon. My mom says it's more fun when there is a group of us. She is actually right on that one, but I'm surprised she admits it, given that being in groups brings out the bad in boys.

In the basement for a serious Nerf duel, all six of us, and we've got a game! It's two on four, Henry and Josh against everyone else since they're the oldest and biggest. Nerf bullets are flying everywhere, and we're diving for cover behind chairs, under the ping-pong table, and over the bean bag "bunkers." The old mattress (gross actually) and tons of blankets make a fort, walls and tents.

The sweet basement battleground we make is an extreme no-man's land of survival of the fittest. The basement seems to shake as we hurl ourselves over the obstacles, onto the floor or land in a human pile-up against the walls. Grunts, groans and warrior cries fill the air.

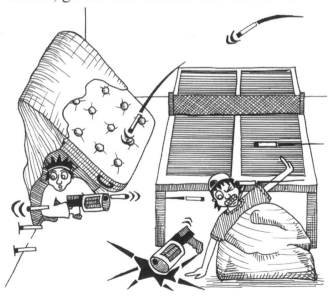

The killing is going hilariously well until Henry gets started. "Charlie, what're you doing? That was too close, it hurt, man!"

Charlie had nailed Henry in the face, ouch, and he couldn't care less. "What're you a pretty boy? Game on, suck it up, let's go!"

The basement stops it's whirling on a dime and the wicked and wild fun drops to dead silence. No one says anything. No one moves.

A real fight is on. Fighting in front of friends embarrasses me.

"Shut up," Henry yells at Charlie.

Oh man, shut up is a giant, monster way to get in trouble in our house. Sure enough, incoming. Mom is blasting her way downstairs. She's like a tornado gathering energy as she spins eagerly toward touching down. We all freeze and take cover. One by one, each of us rises up for a peak like a prairie dog popping out of his hole.

" Outside. All of you up. Time to take this outside!" she says, in the marine sergeant mom voice.

"Ah, Mom it's raining, remember?" I say, still so bummed that my idiot brothers ruined the Nerf war that I risk firing up Mom even more.

"I know, but that's just tough darts", says Mom. "You guys blew it."

Without an option, in a split second we go from timid prairie dogs to stampeding antelope. The herd of six runs up the stairs, and into the garage. We all play lacrosse, so that's what it's going to be.

"Three v three?" Henry says.

We're all cool with that. Of course, Charlie plays goalie because he really is a goalie. A good goalie. That plus he craves being the center of the action—understandable, yes, but still obnoxious.

"JJ, you play goalie too," Charlie instructs me. No choice on this one. I know I can't protest cause they'll start hitting me harder, or something. They suit me up in Charlie's old pads so I'm real covered, feeling more like an actor in a fat suit than an athlete because the pads are so bulky. Being inside all of this huge stuff makes me feel like I'm inside myself! No one else has pads on. They just have sticks and gloves. I can hardly move

with these huge pads, but I waddle out like
a stumbling robot to the backyard. Yup, still
raining a little bit.... just enough for everything
to be slippery.

The only rule in backyard lacrosse is that
there are no rules. Unfortunately, with no rules,
anything can happen and almost everything
does. Henry and Josh are monsters compared

to Troy and me. They shoot the ball eighty miles per hour and now they're aiming at ME! Shoot to kill. They don't care; they just want to throw the ball hard and see the resulting probability of pain. This is not going well and I'm thinking back to the piranha in the goldfish tank. Be tough, be tough, be tough ...I have to do this. Then suddenly, I have a perfect thought and I am thinking hey, this may work out: If I play goalie now and miss every ball..........I let every ball that's got a snowball's chance go by me (shouldn't be a stretch!) and go right into the net....Charlie will see that I actually stink in goal. And SNAP! I am back to cruising on attack, conversation, and debate OVER! Brilliant!

"Hurry up guys, let's go," Charlie says, bossing us all around like usual. I know I must be bugging him by really taking my sweet time! As they say, little brothers can be the Masters of being a pain!

"Game on," Henry says as he whips the ball to his friend Josh. Josh catches it and cradles it right handed, then left handed and back to right handed. I'm just waiting for that ball to explode right at me. This is not the kind of lacrosse that leads to a long life. Should I drop to the ground or just stand here? I close my eyes and wait for the shells to hit.

"Shoot. Shoot on Jake!" Charlie yells at Josh who has the ball.

Here comes the heavy artillery. I'm getting ready for a pounding. The first ball whizzes right by my right ear, I think, because I don't know for real; yup, closed my eyes.

"Okay Jake, you can do this, be quick, watch the ball," Charlie says

Oh yeah, I'm watching the ball all right, watching it go right by me into the net! Dan shoots next, but it careens off the pipe. His force vibrates the goal. Ben shoots again. I shift slightly left, and score for the other guys, exactly according to my plan.

"Use your body, get in front of it," Charlie yells out. "Get in front of it and step into it." Who's he kidding? Not me, cause I'm stepping right out of this goalie thing. There will be no stepping into it!

I manage to drop three more shots and make one real save, only because it was a perfect shot to my stick. But, Charlie is not buying it.

"Come on Jake, you can do this, step up, man," he says. Then he adds, "Or should I say little boy." Charlie is a regular riot.

"Hot cookies," Mom's call triggers my relief. When Mom

bakes, Troy the food guy can't be contained. Thankfully, the action stops, sticks and gloves litter the ground. We're all ready for a break.

Before I finish my first hot, melting, most-awesome chocolate-chip cookie, Charlie is back on me with the goalie propaganda.

"So, wasn't it crazy great Jake? Balls flying from out of nowhere right past your ears makes you just feel so alive out there, right?" Charlie asks, but it's really more of a statement, like he's watching himself star in his own dream.

Alive, huh? Like how you feel alive in midair after jumping off a building.

"Charlie, I stunk. Didn't you see? I only made one save. Were you even there? Face it—I stunk. I have always stunk. I do stink. I will stink. You just be the Jennings Goalie. It's just not happening for me. Got it?" There, I've actually told him. I'm scared, but it feels good.

I'm bracing for the fury, the lecture, and the explosion.

"Nah, just more practice, and you'll get there," he replies calmly. Good grief! Did he not hear anything I said? Maybe Charlie's taken more hits to the head than I'd realized.

Still, all in all, not a bad day: Six guys, a gnarly basement Nerf battle, and a little Lax that actually ended in some out-of-control mud sliding.

TEN

Practice– Hot Rock

"Hey Troy, where's Ricky?" I'm asking as we walk to the field with one more game and three weeks left in our season.

"Don't know," Troy answers. "Wait, there he is up there—come on let's catch up to him."

Troy, Ricky and I just start bouncing into each other, spinning with every check like we're a living pinball game, and dropping the ball while we're at it. The whistle sends us running to Coach.

"Guys, today we're playing a drill called Hot Rock. It's a 2 on 3 drill. See the squares made by the cones on the field? You'll have three attack against two defenders in each square. The three attackers pass the "hot rock" around to see how many passes they can complete in 30 seconds. Defenders, one covers the ball, the other one covers the man and you see how many turnovers you can force

in 30 seconds. Okay, let's go. Remember, scoop, don't rake those ground balls. Keep the balls in the sticks and move your feet!"

Coach blows the whistle. Troy, Ricky and I start on attack and we're passing. It's hard. I've got the ball, but Tank is on me. Bam, he swats my stick, ball down. Darn! He's got it and is out of the square. I hear the whistle, turn around and there is Coach.

"Good hustle, Patel. Jake, you've got to cradle and dodge to keep possession," Coach says.

Darn, I think, can't Coach ever catch me doing something right?

"Okay, guys, carry on, and keep passing that hot rock," Coach barks, and the chaos resumes.

Sure enough, just as Coach walks away, we catch on fire! Ricky fires to me perfectly. Ben gets on me in a flash. I actually spin away and get a pass to Ricky who fires to Troy. He's got it, cradles, and then back to me. Four completions! I sneak a look at the pocket on my stick cause I'm not always sure the ball is really there. The whistle blows. Coach yells, "Bring it in, gentlemen. Ricky, Troy, Jake, Ben and Patel, you guys stay." "Do we stink or are we amazing?" I think to myself.

"Watch the follow- through in this sequence. Pass to your target and your feet should always be moving. Go ahead, guys."

The whole team is watching and, yup, I drop the first "hot rock." Ricky is on it, and sends it to Troy, and back to me. We're all in motion. Ben is all over me, but I manage to get it back to Ricky. It looks like Tank will intercept, but Ricky dodges and catches the pass. He immediately fires back to Troy for four passes. We've done it! Ricky makes us all look good. Such a sweet sequence!

Coach blows the whistle again. "Great play guys. That's what I'm talking about. You guys are really playing some ball now just in time for our last regular season game. After that we wrap up our season with the Indian Tournament in two weeks. Your hard work's paid off. Now you can cradle, throw, catch, scoop, and dodge. All of these practice drills help you experience game-like situations. This combination of skills and experience will make you good, maybe even great lacrosse players—especially if you make the stick your double. Like your twin you do everything together your stick, even sleep with it. Always, always, always have that stick in your hand. And keep a bucket of balls nearby in case your twin gets hungry."

"Coach," Ben interjects, "I just got a lax bounce back wall in my backyard!"

"That's great, Ben, I can just see you out there with all of those sisters in your house. That lax wall is like the brother you never had!"

We're all rolling on the ground laughing at that one.

ELEVEN

Charlie's Out!

As I grabbed my bag and packed up my equipment from this week's practice, Ricky and his mom find me.

"Hey Jake, you're coming home with us!" Ricky announces.

"Your house, on a school night? Amazing!" This seemed a little strange. My mom always preaches homework first, and she stalks me like prey until I'm finished. Confused, I look at Ricky's mom.

"So where is my mom?" I ask.

"Your brother fell at school and she had to take him for an X-ray of his ankle," Ricky's mom informs me.

"Henry or Charlie, what happened?" Ricky asked. He wants to know too.

"Charlie, I think. I don't know the whole story except that his ankle got so swollen that the nurse insisted that he needed an X-ray,"  she answers. Ricky's mom's voice had that distant tone adults have where you know you're not getting the whole story, but that's all you're going to get. "How bad is he?" I wonder. "Is his lax season shot?"

Before I can ask another question, Ricky's mom is on her cell with my mom.

"Looks like I'll be taking you home. That was your mom, and they're home."

"What about his season?" Ricky asks.

"Yeah, he is gonna be so bummed," I say.

"They only have a few more games until the state tournament. This is not gonna be good."

Riding home I wonder what did this mean to me. Is he going to be all cranky and mad and take it out on me, bossing me around even more? Bummer for Charlie, but this has bummer for Jake written all over it!

"See you tomorrow Ricky, thanks for the ride Mrs. Shaw," I say getting out of the car.

"Mom, Charlie, where are you guys?" I ask, bursting through the back door.

"In here, Jake," Mom says meaning the family room. I run into the room, but freeze right there. All I see is this big bright pink cast resting on the table.

"Pink, Charlie, you have a bright pink cast," I say. I can't believe it. For once, I am speechless.

"Yeah, it's beyond macho. But Dude, how about trying, are you okay? What happened?" Charlie replies.

I really don't care. I just can't stop staring at the pink beacon. We're guys right? Pink is just not a Jennings color!

Just then Dad comes home.

"Pink? Sweet choice, Charlie! How's it feel? " Dad says. Could my Dad really think pink is sweet?

"Yeah, its sweet isn't it, hah! When I was leaving school, Maggie and Elizabeth bet me $10 that I wasn't man enough to get a pink cast. So, I guess I am now $10 richer!"

Charlie actually sounds pretty pleased with this fact. It is a relief to know that he didn't really choose pink but I'm beginning to see the advantage of pink for him: girl appeal.

"How long for the cast?" my father asks.

"The doctor said he broke the growth plate in his ankle, a very common injury. In fact they'll take it off in three weeks," Mom explains.

"Dad this is really, really bad," Charlie starts, "We have three more games until the state tournament, and we have to win at least one of them to qualify! My team needs me! What are we going to do? I mean I should be okay by the tournament, but how can we find another goalie at this stage of the season?

Maybe I can play with the cast on," Charlie is starting to get all worked up.

"No! Right now you need to stay off that ankle and let your coach work out how to protect the goal. Now, tell me about those stairs," Dad instructs.

Charlie chuckles, "Oh yeah, I tried to skip a few steps and didn't quite make it to the bottom."

"Charlie! Jumping stairs? You bozo. What were you thinking?" Dad questions.

"What I was thinking was that I really should have had a running start!" Charlie exclaims.

"Not the answer I was looking for," my dad adds with a sigh.

So Charlie's out for the next month. He's on crutches, and can't get around. I'm thinking that the goalie pressure is off. Now he can focus on his own team and leave me alone! But, tomorrow is game day for us again, so we'll see.

TWELVE

Game #7–Timmy!

Game day. Our last game before the famous Indian Tournament, which is the end of our season. Coach Morgan blows his almighty whistle (Yup, I finally know his name).

"Okay guys, our last game until…" That's when I blacked out because all I heard after "until" was "Mikey in goal." I'd beaten the odds by actually avoiding goalie yet again. Yes! Even better it was Mikey's turn in goal. Ha! No showing off for him today. But then I returned to planet earth because Troy was elbowing me.

"YO, J., wake up, dude. You're Captain!" Captain, not goalie, the last game. Double yes! I jogged to the middle of the field to meet the ref and shake hands with the guy from the other team, feeling very official to be representing my team for the last game.

"Come down, get real, Jake," I had to say to myself. The referee whistles the game to life and Troy has the face-off. I'm downfield, back on defense. They've got the ball; their attack is moving in. They fire a pass and complete another. Granted it's only the last regular season game, but we're finally down with the three passes to shoot rule!

"Who has the hole?" I hear Coach yell. I'm on it; got it, the spot right in front of the goal, ready to get in the way of the next pass, shot or body. Bammo! My guy has the ball. I'm trying to anticipate his next move. He attempts a bull dodge, rolling shoulders and using his head and shoulders to protect his stick. I'm almost beaten but in desperation I check his stick and block the potential shot on goal.

"Ball down," all of the parents are yelling like the crazies the game makes them.

"Oh man," I hear the other kid say, "I almost had that one." That voice sounded familiar, but how? I'm not sure. No time to think about that. I've got the ball on the outside and manage a pass to Ben. Phew, now it's up to the guys on attack.

I go back to my position in front of the goal and that attack guy on the other team is moving over to me. What is it with this kid? He won't leave me alone. He keeps looking at me and it's a little creepy. Ben's got the ball and one, two, three, Tank shoots and misses. So goes the action until we hit halftime at 0-0.

Quick break; helmets and gloves off. Coach talks, nobody hears. Helmets and gloves on. I look over at the other team and just catch that kid with the familiar voice putting his helmet on. It's Timmy, my buddy from the summer. We swim on a team together. No wonder he sounded familiar. Timmy! I'm actually guarding Timmy, and he's not actually creepy. The two of us are half of the same freestyle relay team. No way. Small world. Dang, this is cool!

Jimmy takes the faceoff and we're moving again. Still on D, specifically, I'm on Timmy!

"Yo, Timmy, I didn't know you play lacrosse."

"J.J., my man, what's going on? I didn't know you play either," Timmy responds.

"Are you swimming again this summer?"

"Yeah, how about you?"

"Definitely," I say.

Before we can say anything else, we both look up as the ball is flying right at us.

"Timmy, pay attention," his coach is yelling.

"J.J., wake up out there," my coach is on me now, too.

Timmy receives the ball, but I'm on him quickly. He switches to one hand, brings his stick in an arch over my head to his other hand, gets both hands back on, shoots and scores. A split second later I'm lying on top of him. Too late. The two of us are helmet to helmet looking at each other.

"Hey, Dude, why did you have to ruin our reunion by scoring?" I call over to him.

"Beats me. That ball just landed in my stick then flew into the goal," he laughs. "Besides you should have known that I am the king of the swim move."

Yeah, I should have known that being a swimmer; Timmy might have perfected that move.

"Hey, it's my Mojo, I can't help it if I'm a stud," Timmy laughs.

"Mojo, what the heck?" I ask. We're both cracking up.

The whistle blows. Tank's got the faceoff. It flies in Troy's direction, but not into his stick. Scoop, he's got it, off to Ricky, then to Ben, he shoots, he scores! Tie game, 1-1. I'm relieved and feeling my Mojo rising!

Then they get the ball. One long pass and it's flying all the way to Timmy, but this time I'm the one who's quick. I scoop, run up, and send it back to Ben. Pass, pass, pass, rocket launch, and the ball bounces off the post – so close! We're all dropping the ball everywhere. I'm still thinking about Timmy and Mojo, when once again, the ball is whizzing in our direction. They're passing behind the goal. We're all moving; Timmy and I are pushing each other as hard as we can. Here it comes again, back to center, back to Timmy. This time I'm ready and refuse to be beaten by Timmy's almighty swim move. I'm on him, on the ball. He can't get a shot off, the whistle blows and the game ends 1-1.

"Man, J.J., I thought I had that. Can't you even let a guy get a goal?" Timmy is breathing hard and sounding kind of hurt.

"I guess it's my Mojo," I shout back. Then we're both rolling on the grass again cracking up. "See you this summer, man," I say.

"Yeah," Timmy says. "I hope your freestyle is better than your lax game, ha, ha." He gets in the last word before we both turn back to our teams. Swim team, lacrosse, I wonder where Timmy will show up next.

Charlie seems to be letting up on the goalie harassment. Besides with only the tournament left to play, I'm thinking I might make it through the entire season playing only backyard goalie.

THIRTEEN

Tournament Training

It's God's greatest gift to mankind: Friday! Tomorrow the Indian Tournament begins. Troy, Ricky and Ben are coming over so we can practice before the big day.

Pumped up to the max, we pile out of the car. Henry and Charlie head straight inside. No time for snacks. Troy, Ricky, Ben and I are putting on our gloves and grabbing our sticks for some back yard 2 on 2. Ben and I vs. Ricky and Troy. We run around for a while, basically playing Keep Away. Charlie arrives on the scene. He's now off his crutches and walking on his puke pink cast. What does he want? These are my friends, at our house to hang with me— not Charlie.

"Hey guys, want me to set up some cones and a course around the yard?" Charlie asks.

"Ah, Charlie, we're kind of ..." I start to say. If only Charlie were a girl, then he'd be more interested in Barbies and stupid clothes stuff instead of ruling my life.

Troy interrupts, "sounds hardcore."

"Yeah", Ricky and Ben chimed in. Before I know it, Charlie is in charge of not only me, but my friends too. Strange thing, they actually seem okay with this, so I have no choice but to go along. But Charlie being Charlie, he'd actually thought out a pretty great plan.

"Okay guys. It's going to be like Frisbee golf in teams. Each team takes turns picking a tree; then your partner runs to the tree to catch a pass. Whoever gets to the tree and completes the pass first gets a point."

"Charlie, this is genius," I blurt out. I can't believe it. What an awesome game and I think I just called my dumb brother a genius. I surprise myself quite a lot, but surprising myself still surprises me every time.

We play lacrosse Frisbee golf for a while. Then, as usual, Troy is starving. We all race inside. Charlie is with us, too. My mom always has great snacks when we have friends over. Today it was an entire box of soft pretzels with cinnamon dip. Mom loves our friends anytime, but she loves them even more when she fills them up!

"Mrs. J., these pretzels rock," says Troy as he walks to the counter to fill up his cup with Gatorade. "Oh, do you have the Sharpie to put our name on the cups?"

"You always have the Sharpie out, Mrs. J.," Ricky adds.

Did someone ask for a Sharpie? It's my mom in her element, in Sharpie heaven.

Henry smells the pretzels and joins the feeding frenzy.

"So you guys have the big Indian Tournament tomorrow. That's the real deal. Those were the days. I think that's the tournament that gives out trophies," Henry says.

I don't have
a lacrosse trophy,
and I want one.
Badly. I'm picturing
it on my shelf next
to my soccer and
swimming medals.
Filling up that shelf
is a personal goal of
mine.

INDIAN TOURNAMENT
CHAMPION

Henry looks at Charlie and says, "Hey
Chuck, how about you and I take these guys out
back and drill them for the tournament? You
can feed passes so you don't have to run on Mr.
Pinkie."

This is very confusing. Is my 15-year-
old, X-box champion, girl-charming, brother
suggesting to my 12-year-old, can-create-
anything brother that they actually play with us?
Unbelievable, but I can't stop thinking there's
a catch. But no, Charlie is in, and said nothing

to do with playing goalie! I must be in another house. No, make that another planet in a parallel universe.

Charlie says, "Yo, Troy. Whenever you're finished stuffing those pretzels in your mouth, grab your gear. See you out back."

"Okay guys. Let's work on fast breaks," Henry suggests.

"Imagine if you kids could ever out hustle, or even out run us. Of course that would never happen, but that's what you need to think. I know its tough for those measly 10-year-old brains to focus, but focus guys, focus." Henry's words of wisdom.

We played and played. We dodged the trees as if they were players, ran around the house, around the tree fort, around the soccer balls in the yard and even up and down the hill. Yamaha ran around us, his tail twirling like our sticks. I was tired and sweaty in that good way that makes you know you'll remember this time forever. This was a blast and Charlie and Henry were playing with us, not at us or in spite of us. We were all playing together. It was perfection.

Dad drove up in his car and looked astonished; having the same thoughts I had no doubt. He just stood and watched.

"Looks good, gang. Troy, Jake, Ben, Ricky, looks like the Chiefs are ready for the tournament."

"You know we're ready," Ricky says overflowing with confidence.

"We're pumped, Mr. Jennings," Troy said breathing hard.

"You guys look great, but save some juice for tomorrow. How about a break?"

Contentedly, we all collapsed on the patio.

"How did the game go Charlie?" Dad asked.

"Oh, Dad, it's really bad. We lost again. You've got to let me play. I can walk on the cast now. Besides Coach tried and we can't come up with another goalie and our backup stinks! Come on Dad, one more game, one more loss and we miss our shot at States." Charlie is seriously begging.

"This is tough, really tough, but no, you can't play on it until the doctor says its okay," Dad responds in that commanding way that always ends the discussion on the spot.

Defeated, Charlie looks at me, "I always thought you'd be a goalie, little brother. Too bad, with just a little more training, I could have made you a real player!"

"Charlie, there are other positions," I begin, but he cuts me off.

"Yeah, but nothing like goalie, the backbone of the defense. You really missed your shot on this one," he told me, as if my life had taken a wrong turn from which it could never recover.

Still, being the backbone of the defense sounded pretty cool. He almost had me thinking about it for half a second. But nope, I'm sticking with my dreams, unless Coach makes me play goal, and he probably won't because we only have the tournament left so he'll totally use someone with experience. Right?

And that's how the day ended. Charlie invented lax-style Frisbee golf. Henry and Charlie drilled us and they got really sweaty because we "measly" 10-year-olds ran them around. We all had the kind of fun you can never plan. Brothers can be cool. Lacrosse? Always cool.

FOURTEEN

The Tournament: The Best Game Ever

We wake up at 6 a.m. to get to the tournament by 7 a.m. Our warm-ups start at 7:30, but Coach, being a world-class warrior, had us all meet at 7. We drive to the tournament, but the place is so huge that we take a bus from the parking lot to the fields. Lacrosse fields stretch as far as you can see. Like a giant parade, except with no one watching, the people enter carrying coolers, gear bags, chairs, tents and even bags of ice. The whole spectator scene is a sport itself, and the parents' part is to show off the best spread.

We find the Chief's spot easily. Coach had already set up this huge tent that says "Chiefs Lacrosse Club" on the side. It all feels so incredibly important, like I am going to Henry or Charlie's tournament, but this one is for me. Dad carries our ridiculously huge cooler to the tent. We brought all the colors of the Gatorade rainbow: blue, orange, yellow, purple, and red. The tent is big enough for a big table

and lots of folding chairs. Soon Troy shows up with a huge box of sports bars. Ricky kicks in homemade chocolate cookies. Ben provides fruit and Mikey adds chips. But despite all of the deliciousness of the food, we are all too psyched to feel hungry although Troy eyes the spread pretty seriously.

"Yo, check out Mikey's new stick," Ben calls to us.

"Are you kidding me? A new stick for the last games of the season?" I'm trying to complain to Troy but the stick is too darn tempting. We have to check it out. If money can't buy happiness, you'd never know it from watching us surround that new stick. What else could the kid possibly get?

"It's made with a special pocket just for attack," Mikey brags. "It's the Swizzle shaft with the Viper head, pretty sweet combo, huh?"

"Man that does look pretty radical," Ben comments.

"Yeah, looking to score big with this bad boy," Mikey just can't resist boasting one more time.

Still, I'm really eyeing his new weapon. I've learned the stick is key. I don't want to admit it, but once again Mikey's stuff is so hot it's cool.

"We Are the Champions" blares on the loud speakers. It's already over 80 degrees before the sun even gets its game on; today is going to be a real scorcher. Cones and spray paint mark at least a dozen battlefields where we need to win three straight games to make it to the finals. With twenty teams in our division, the finals seem as far away from the present as the beginning of the season.

Coach calls us together. He's acting all formal today, and we can tell from his seriousness that even he's nervous.

"Okay, Chiefs. This is it. We're four, one and one. A great record. We can do this. We've prepared, and we're ready. Before we head out in a few minutes to warm up, everybody line up. It's time for war paint," he instructs.

Like real Indian Chiefs preparing for battle, he spreads real eye-black under our eyes. We look so fierce. We look how we feel. The

most amazing day ever is climbing higher and higher with the sun.

Revved up like Corvette engines for our game, we all sprint to field number 10. Then the music stops playing and a super loud horn sounds the beginning of the action. We win the first game 5 to 2. Troy was in goal. Ben, Ricky, and A.J. score. But not Mikey, he just couldn't score despite the Swizzle-Viper combo. All sweaty already, we run back to the tent to attack the food and drinks in celebration. We wolf down the spread with the appetite of successful hunters.

"Okay, guys, let's just relax. We have two hours until our next game," Coach says. "You can check out the speed ball competition over there, but the main thing you need to do is cool down and rest up."

Ricky jumps up and leads the way. Ben, Troy and I follow with our dads behind us. If there is anything better than awesome this is it:

a huge net surrounds a goal with a backboard in it. Each player has three balls to shoot and score for the fastest shot. Ricky shoots first: 53 miles per hour. When the ball hits the board, it makes a loud smack sound that has me jumping each time. Troy scores 49 and Ben 46. My turn next. I fiercely launch the first ball. It flies over the target by two feet. What a loser. The next two balls hit and I finish behind Ricky at 51.

Most impressive of all is that my dad convinced Ricky's dad, the lacrosse legend, to give it a try. His first ball hits so hard we all drop to the ground.

"Wow, Ricky. Your dad shoots with authority. He really is a legend," I say.

Ricky's Dad's best ball tops 90 miles per hour. Imagine playing goalie against him-YIKES! Good-bye head!

"Man, that is better than any carnival game ever," I say.

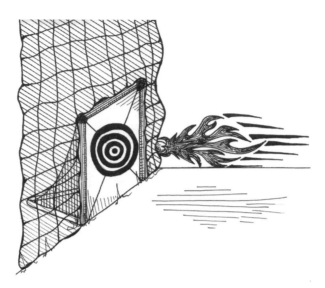

"Yeah," Troy agrees. "Let's go back and see what else there is to eat."

"Seriously, Troy, how can you still be hungry? Do they actually feed you at home?"

The horn blasts again bringing us back on the field. This game is tougher still, 0 to 0 at the half. Coach put Patel in at center and he wins the face off. Mikey has the ball on the third pass. Although once again he quickly fakes left and goes right, he shoots and misses embarrassingly. Ricky intercepts from the defense, passes to Troy, instantly back to Ricky and then to me. I shoot and score! Oh man, what a feeling. Three perfect passes and a perfect shot.

"Yeah, JJ! Way to go," I heard from the Chief's fans.

Thirty seconds to go. Patel wins the faceoff again. He passes to me, I shovel it to Troy. After bringing his stick to his opposite side, keeping his eyes forward and stepping across, Troy continues to move away from the rushing defense. He reverses it over to Mikey who shoots and misses again. What is with Mikey? He can usually always score. Maybe his stick is cursed. The buzzer blasts and the game is over.

We are screaming and high fiving each other. We win the game, only 1 to 0. My goal is feeling even better now than when it happened.

We qualify for the semi-final round. I am totally floating on pride.

Back at the tent, the shade welcomes us. The sun is reaching lethal intensity. Tank is panting like a dog. We grab handfuls of ice to eat and rub all over our red-hot faces which turns into a huge ice chucking, kinda hurting crazy free-for-all. Soaked now from ice and sweat, we have attitude.

"Enough, Chiefs. Cool it," Coach bellows.

I guess our attitude doesn't seem so cool to him.

We all sit down and eat some more. I am beginning to feel like Troy with the bottomless stomach. Before we can even ask to go back to the shooting area, the horn blows again. We are headed to the semi-finals.

FIFTEEN

The Finals:
The Best Day Ever

This game is against the Twisters. Coach asked me to take the face off, a possible reward for the game-winning goal in the last game. My first face off and the second to last game of the season. It's all good, especially since I win the face off – so hot on myself – but then I drop the ball and the Twisters get it. Thank goodness The Tank is there and we take possession again. After an exhausting back and forth half with the Twisters, we're tied. The first half ends 2 to 2.

The second half begins with me on defense, and the Twisters keep yelling "go to X." When they say that, one player goes behind the goal and passes it up to a player on either side of the goal. It's hard to know who to guard.

The Twisters are good at this formation. We manage to hold them off until Mikey finally re-finds his shooting talent. It's a Troy, Ricky, Mikey combo that finally scores. Playing tough—really tough—the Chiefs win again!

We make the finals of the Indian Tournament. As we're slapping hands at the end of the game, I notice that Mikey has his old stick in his hand now. Interesting.

As we make our way through the crowds and back to the tent, I look up to see Henry and Charlie. What are they doing here?

"Hey J., heard you scored a game winner in round two. Now you're in the finals. Way to go little bro!" Henry says.

"Give me five," Charlie says.

"What are you guys doing here?" I question.

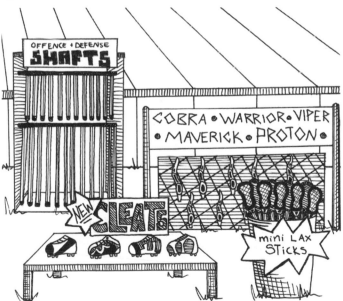

"Came to watch our little bro make us proud," Charlie responds.

"Have you checked out the vendors?" Henry asks.

"Vendors? What's that?" I say.

"It's like a bunch of lacrosse stores in tents all together," he replies.

My brothers have actually come to watch my tournament, and now they're offering to take me with them to vendor heaven.

"Let's go. Bring your buddies. It's the best. They sell supreme stuff: stringing kits, sticks, gloves, t-shirts, shorts, sweats and even tape." Henry offers.

So off we go, Troy, Ricky, A.J. and me. It is decidedly cool. Of course, I'd seen what I thought was a lot of ultimate lax stuff with Henry and Charlie, but this is like Santa's workshop, all lax! Immediately Henry finds a shirt he really wanted that says, "If you can't play nice, play lacrosse." Anything for a laugh with him. Charlie, of course, can't stop inspecting the head-stringing kits, his new specialty. We Chiefs handle and inspect just about everything there.

Still high on just the smell of all that new lax gear, we return just in time for Coach's last pep talk of the season.

"I am so proud of you, Chiefs. Now you cradle, throw, catch, scoop, dodge and play defense with domination. You now know the moves of the fastest game on two feet. Here we go; it's our last game, the finals. Let's give it all we've got. Jake, I think we'll try you in goal. I've been saving you all season for this," Coach instructs. "I know you'll be a natural just like your brother!"

CANCEL BEST DAY EVER! ENTER WORST DAY EVER!

Unbelievable. I went from totally pumped to totally devastated in one millisecond. What's he mean saving me, like from what? Dang. Our last game and I'm in goal. Charlie and Henry help me put on my goalie gear. They know what I'm thinking.

"Ok Jake. You can do this," Henry says.

"Come on Jake, just like in the yard, get in the zone," Charlie adds. I realize Charlie still hasn't given up on converting me.

They both slap me high fives. Their support helps a little. Maybe. Ok, maybe a lot.

The horn blows, and we're jogging out for the championship game. The Chiefs start practicing shots on me. When I look down field – unbelievable, I'm stunned. It's the Warriors. And wearing number sixteen is Timmy, my best friend from swim team, who, by the way, has the hardest shot in the league and it's soon to be aimed directly at me – uh-oh! Suddenly my deep dark secrets about having to play goalie hijack my mind! I am terrified. This is it. I just wish that I wasn't "it"! Could it get any worse? Now I'm no longer a random goldfish in the safety of the school with the other goldfish but instead that lowly single, lonely, bottom-feeder fending for himself.

After warm-ups, I'm thinking I may not be quite as near death as I'd feared, but close. Sure enough, Coach is there and starts firing at me. It's not backyard goalie anymore. This is it. Do or Die. Win or Lose. Live ammunition. But, surprisingly, I'm still actually standing. I'm okay. The pads seem to be working. Maybe I can be tough. I'm doing my little robot dance in the crease and actually stopping shot after shot. In the backyard, I didn't even try. I mean, I even closed my eyes. But here, I really focus on the ball and quickly discover that I'm a half way decent goalie.

The whistle blows. Game on. And right off, here comes Timmy; he's playing center attack and parking right in front of me.

"That you Jennings?" Timmy mumbles through his facemask.

"Yeah. I've got my goalie Mojo," I reply, trying to keep my eyes on the sweeping action at the other end of the field.

"Aw, you play like my Grandma," Timmy cracks.

We both kind of force a laugh, but this is no time for fun and games with the enemy. A split second later, Timmy has the ball. He turns to face me and I move left. He dodges right, and rips it right past me into the goal. The Warriors are up 1 to 0 in the first minute of the game. I'm devastated. But I'm also a Chief and this is war.

The rest of the first half rolls back and forth. It feels like the Warriors are shooting every minute. Bring it on. I snag one, kick one, block two, but then let another in. The two minute whistle blows. It's tied at 3 to 3, but not for long: the Warriors score again—Nooooo . I'm swinging my stick, banging the posts on the frame of the net, half out of anger, and half just trying to make some noise to get the guys going.

Our attack is charged. Patel, Jimmy, Mikey are passing great and even catching great. But, maybe not quite on fire, Ricky keeps shooting like a champ, but we can't seem to get the ball in the goal. Back to his old stick, Mikey is hot again, but still even he can't score. The clock is ticking. Will we have time to get on the board? At last Ricky reaches back and sends one in. It's 4 to 4 with just a few seconds left. Patel is now playing defense and guarding Timmy. He is so close to him that he misses another Warrior breaking away down the field. The Warrior shoots and the whistle blows to end the game. I turn around to see the ball behind me in the goal. The reality that the Chiefs are history feels like something good has died. It has. The Warriors killed it by winning the Indian Tournament.

We line up to shake hands after the game. The Warriors are all smiles, teeth shining bright like the sun. I lower my eyes to avoid the look of victory in their glare, until suddenly, I hear Timmy's voice.

"Yo, Jennings. Great game. You rock in goal," he says.

"Yeah J.J. You had the best saves of the season," Ben says.

"You did it all," Ricky adds. "Stick saves, kick saves, and even over-the-shoulder saves. You're a natural man."

I still can't face my own team. I've let them down. We lost. I let the last ball in. I feel like I could puke or cry, but I really can't do either. I'm that bummed. The funny thing is,

I actually liked playing goalie. It was quick, action packed and intense. I felt super alive and real—like the difference between watching a game live compared to on TV. Yup, I, Jake Jasper Jennings, loved goalie!

Over at the sidelines Charlie's eye catches me. He's up to something. He's jumping all over in front of my Dad who's on his cell phone. What's with that?

"Amazing, brilliant, outstanding," Coach told us. "You Chiefs all played a great game. Each of you contributed. We don't have just one MVP, we have AVPs- All Valuable Players. Now we have the secret formula for our success: Mikey for face offs, Ricky for center attack with Ben and Troy on the wings, Patel on Defense, and Jake in goal. You Chiefs are destined to be next year's power house."

We lost and it sucks (not supposed to use that word, but that's how it feels right now). Coach gives us each our runner-up trophy. My mood improves. Second place, but a trophy is a trophy.

I shake Coach's hand and say, "Thanks, Coach Morgan, for being our Coach this year. Lacrosse is awesome." I think he is impressed that I finally remembered his name.

"Thank you, Jake. You're off to a great start. Hope to see you for many more years on the field and hopefully in the goal," he says.

I've recovered. Even better, what I thought would be my nastiest nightmare really turned into a sweet dream! And all of these secrets I had at the beginning of the season don't seem like they need to be secret anymore. I'm alive. I'm a laxer. I'm a goalie.

Before I can take another step, Charlie is in my face.

"Jake, you totally rocked. I knew you had it in you! Where did that come from? Where have you been hiding that...,"obviously my answer didn't matter, because he just keeps yapping.

"So guess what? Dad talked to my Coach, and you're playing up for my team in goal tomorrow, in my place. Isn't that awesome?" he asked.

"Me? Awesome? On your team? What are you talking about," I questioned.

It was all happening so fast, my first season, our first tournament. I dreaded playing goalie an hour ago, now I love it and next I'm goalie on Charlie's team? Even though I'm a lot more than a little confused, no time to hesitate.

There was only one response: "I'm in!"

SIXTEEN

Lifted Up by Playing Up

The whole family arrives at Charlie's game for the early warm up. Charlie's coach walks right over to greet us.

"Hey Jake, thanks so much for helping us out. I heard you put on quite a show at your tournament!" I don't know what to say, but of course Charlie does.

"Let's gear up Jake. The guys can take a few shots on goal to get you ready for the big leagues." Charlie instructs, although it feels like more like a warning.

No turning back now. Here I am, with Charlie's team about to take deadly aim. I feel so far beyond nervous that I'm excited. Charlie,

my new personal coach, signals the firing
squad. They come at me quickly, right, left,
corners, and grounders. The balls are flying. I'm
shifting, deflecting, kicking, and catching. The
hardest of all are the shots that bounce on the
ground then accelerate forward. My team never
shot the ball like that. Focus, watch the ball,
focus, watch the ball, over and over…

The referee blows his whistle, game on. Charlie's team gets possession first and the next thing I know it's halftime, tie score 0-0. Charlie is pacing in front of me like a caged tiger at the zoo. Then, I get it. Charlie is playing goalie too, only through me.

"Awesome. Way to be Jake. You held them that half, one more half to go," Charlie encourages.

"Jake, yeah man, way to go. You own the goal. Jake, you're so hot, you're on fire," I hear familiar voices. I turn to see that this all comes from Ricky, Troy, and Ben.

"Wow…, you're here? Thanks." Seeing my friends, hearing my friends, it is a perfect halftime. They're not on the field playing with me, but the Chiefs are still a team.

Back out there, I'm all pumped up until their center attack shoots hard at the ground right in front of the crease. The ball bounces high over my shoulder and in for a goal. We're losing now, and it's my fault. These guys are the masters of it all: the inside roll, spilt dodges, bull, face and roll dodges, one handed cradling, and changing direction. They cut, pick and dodge with finesse. My job just got harder. Charlie and his team need me even more now.

We score quickly to tie it, 1-1. The clock is ticking. I am focusing on focusing. Charlie's friend Dan fires an amazing shot and putting us up, 2-1.The pressure lightens a little with two minutes to go, because thankfully, our attack dominates. Then possession changes and the other team explodes down the field right at me.

"Steady Jake, watch the ball," Charlie's voice is clear above the rest and puts me in a trance.

They pass around the net, like a pack of wolves looking for the opportunity to strike. Our defense is in the zone, blocking, and checking. The other team sets up the pass and unleashes a shot. The ball is flying to my weak side. Something happens. I move instinctively quickly on the ball with stop-action focus, and catch it over my shoulder. The buzzer sounds, game over. We win! Pure and total exhaustion drop me to the ground right there in front of the ball-empty goal.

Charlie's team scoops me up on their shoulders just like in the NFL on TV! They're all chanting, "Jake, Jake, Jake." So crazy. Everyone dissolves into the cheering, even the

parents. Looking down I realize its Charlie's shoulder I'm sitting on.

"You were so great, Jake. You are a bad to the bone goalie," he says. "Thanks little brother, now we're headed to the State Tournament, thanks to you!"

I look at Charlie and know that this is the best brother moment of my life.

"Sorry it took me so long Charlie," I say.

"Yeah, for a long time, I wanted you to play, but then, I needed you man. I needed you to play," he responds.

Back on the ground, I'm not standing up for too long. Troy, Ricky and Ben all tackle me to the ground before I can move. All I hear are muffled comments like, "You rocked." Their three-on-one tackle was better than a trillion high fives, or anything they could have said. I'm so excited, my heart pounds and little do I know that this best moment is about to get even better.

I look up as my parents are walking over with Henry. Charlie gets up and walks over to Henry and together they're holding a brand new goalie stick with the tag still hanging on the shaft.

"Who got that?" I ask.

"You," they both answer.

"Huh?"

"After that performance in goal today, we thought you might need this for next season," Henry says. "It's the Nemisis with the new Krypto-Pro shaft. Yeah, and what else are we going to spend our allowance on?"

They are smiling so much I almost think it's for them. But that brand new goalie stick is all mine. My brothers actually rock. I'm getting dangerously close to crying. And, now I actually have a sick new stick with the names still printed clearly right there on the shaft.

"Wow, man that is cool." Hmm—a surprise—Mikey had been at the game too. I'm flipping my new stick in my hands, still in shock. Not even Mikey's presence could affect this moment.

"Yo, Jake, that stick is THE best," as if I needed him to confirm that.

"Yeah, it's the best, cause you earned it man, you owned the goal, you played up, and your brothers actually gave it to you……." And then he added, "You know, yeah, way better than anything I ever got." Saying all he needed to say, Mikey just walked off.

My first lacrosse season is over. I got to be captain for a game. I won a faceoff. I didn't win at sprints. I joined my brothers in the lacrosse brotherhood. Ricky, Troy, Ben, the Tank, and yes, even Mikey—together as a team, we have a lot of game in front of us! I may have dropped a few "Hot Rocks" but most importantly, playing the dreaded goalie turned out to be the best thing that ever happened to me. It was also the best thing that ever happened to Charlie and me. And maybe, Dad was right. My old smelly, muddy, used-by-my-brothers equipment worked just fine. It really isn't about the stuff. It's about the guy and the game. I'm the guy, and lacrosse is my game.

Jake Jasper Jennings: Lacrosse Goalie!

Many thanks to the following:

Joy Holmes, and Bridget Flynn, for encouraging me to begin, for helping the concept evolve, and for reading, re-reading, and re-reading.

Ann Reed, who introduced me to Harry Groome.

Harry Groome, who introduced me to George Wattles.

Mom, Kim, Pete, Kathy, Jack, Lori and my cousin Beth's third grade classes.

Tony Garvan, who inspired me to write thirty years ago, for instantly understanding Jake's voice and for his editorial eye. It's been an honor.

My husband Tom, whose incredible support, encouragement, commitment and love of Jake are the backbone of this book.

ABOUT THE AUTHOR

Lisa Butler lives in the heart of Philadelphia's lacrosse country with her team of one husband, three sons and a dog. She openly admits that her favorite stories come from her years on the sidelines. Lisa is forever grateful to all boys for their imagination and energy which enables them to transform an ordinary day into an adventure.

ABOUT THE ILLUSTRATOR

Jacquelyn Dale Whitman (J.D.) is an art student at the University of Chicago. A former lacrosse player who still frequently finds herself with a stick in her hands, J.D. thus far has successfully survived life with three younger brothers.